# INDEX

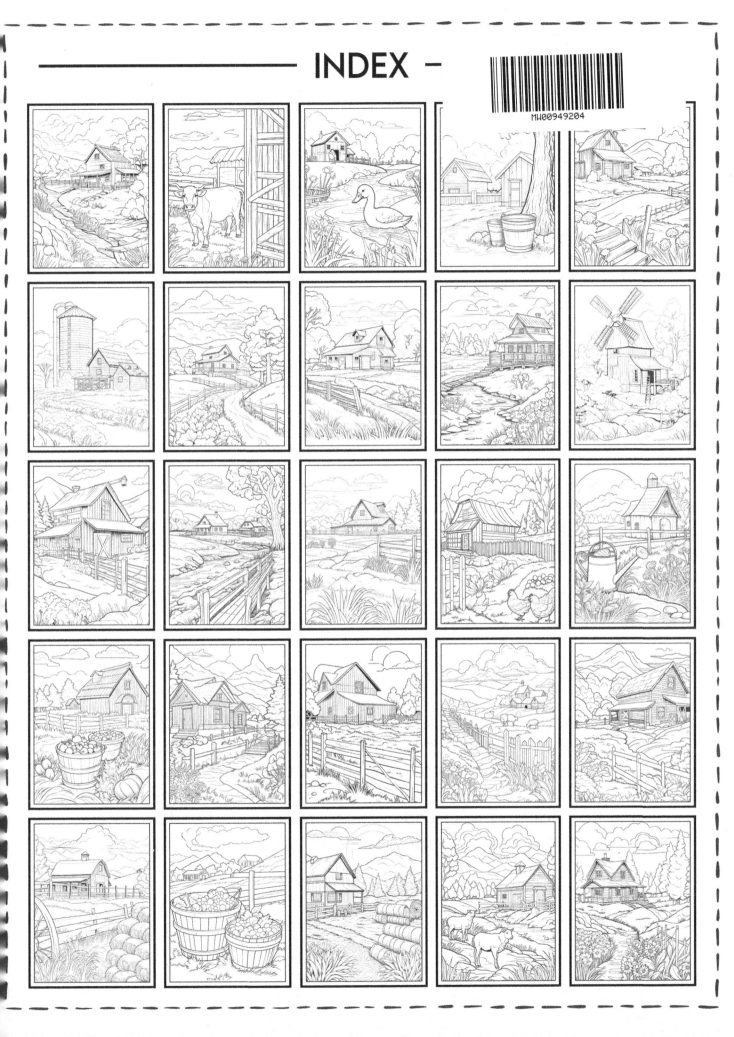

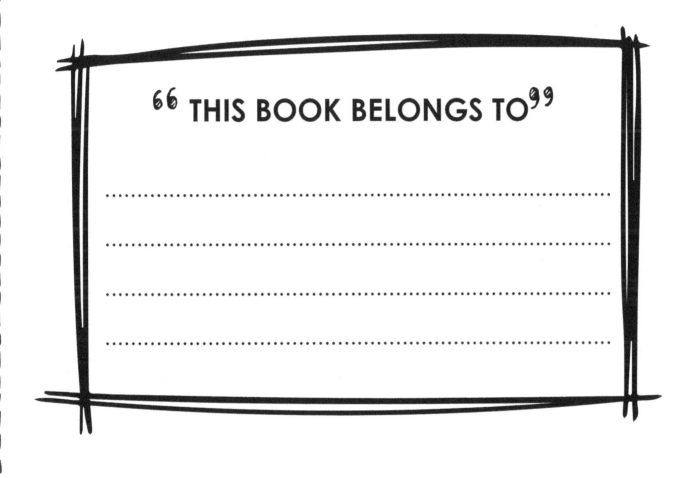

"THIS BOOK BELONGS TO"

.................................................................

.................................................................

.................................................................

.................................................................

# COLOR TEST PAGE

COLOR: _____

COLOR: _____

COLOR: _____

COLOR: _____

COLOR: _____

COLOR: _____

COLOR: _____

COLOR: _____

COLOR: _____

COLOR: _____

COLOR: _____

COLOR: _____

COLOR: _____

COLOR: _____

COLOR: _____

COLOR: _____

COLOR: _____

COLOR: _____

COLOR: _____

COLOR: _____

# WRITE DOWN YOUR FAVORITE ASPECTS
## OF THIS BOOK:

........................................................................................

........................................................................................

........................................................................................

........................................................................................

........................................................................................

........................................................................................

........................................................................................

........................................................................................

........................................................................................

........................................................................................

........................................................................................

........................................................................................

........................................................................................

........................................................................................

........................................................................................

........................................................................................

## THANK YOU FOR TRUSTING US BY PURCHASING OUR BOOKS

Your trust in us means a lot, and we truly hope that you will find joy and satisfaction in coloring our unique designs. If our book meets your expectations, we kindly ask you to leave a positive review as it motivates us to create even better books in the future. Once again, thank you for your support and we hope that our coloring book will bring a little bit of creativity and relaxation into your life.

Made in the USA
Monee, IL
06 December 2023

48386549R00044